Our Rights Online

Monika Davies

Reader Consultants

Brian Allman, M.A.
Classroom Teacher, West Virginia

Cheryl Norman Lane, M.A.Ed.
Classroom Teacher
Chino Valley Unified School District

iCivics Consultants

Emma Humphries, Ph.D.
Chief Education Officer

Taylor Davis, M.T.
Director of Curriculum and Content

Natacha Scott, MAT
Director of Educator Engagement

Publishing Credits

Rachelle Cracchiolo, M.S.Ed., *Publisher*
Emily R. Smith, M.A.Ed., *VP of Content Development*
Véronique Bos, *Creative Director*
Dani Neiley, *Associate Editor*
Fabiola Sepulveda, *Series Designer*

Image Credits: p14 Shutterstock/Tulpahn; p19 Alamy/AB Forces News Collection; p20 Shutterstock/Cristian Dina; p23 Library of Congress[LC-USZ62-107008]; all other images from iStock and/or Shutterstock

TCM Teacher Created Materials
5482 Argosy Avenue
Huntington Beach, CA 92649
www.tcmpub.com

ISBN 978-1-0876-1554-7

Printed by: 51497
Printed in: Taiwan

Table of Contents

Navigating Our Digital World 4

Jump into Fiction:
Online Ready 6

Keep It Private 10

Know Your Boundaries 16

Pair Freedom with Responsibility 22

Stand Up for Your Rights 28

Glossary 30

Index 31

Civics in Action 32

Navigating Our Digital World

Have you ever had a puzzling question you could not figure out? Someone may have told you to "look it up online!" The online world is also known as the internet. The internet is a network of devices across the world. It connects billions of computers. This network allows information to zoom from device to device. Information can move at superspeed online. If you can **access** the internet, a ton of **data** is at your fingertips.

The internet does not just have answers to our questions. People can use the internet to find dinner recipes. Funny cat videos may catch their eye online. People can read newspapers from around the globe. The internet can connect people worldwide. Many people use online messaging services. They can connect with other people almost anywhere. This includes people who live in countries very far away—even across oceans.

The internet has many uses. So, it is important to know how to use this digital world. Every person has rights. Every person also has responsibilities. This is also true online! Let's learn how to explore our digital world safely.

Online Popularity

There are nearly 8 billion people on Earth. In 2020, almost 4.5 billion of them had access to the internet.

Jump into Fiction

Online Ready

It was a Tuesday afternoon, and I'd just gotten home from school. My sister Lucy was on a break from college. I found her curled up on the family sofa. I greeted her by crossing my eyes, and she laughed. Secretly, I was over-the-moon happy to see her back home. My older sister was definitely a responsible adult, but she always made time for me.

"Lizzie-bean, you've got to see this hilarious video," she said.

I plopped down beside her, and she held out her phone, a video lighting up the screen. In it, a cute puppy leapt up—over and over—to catch biscuits, but he kept missing. We giggled at the pup's commitment to catch treats. I asked, "Is this a video on Instagram?"

Lucy nodded, her eyes still glued to her screen.

"Can you show me what you do on there?" I prodded.

Lucy looked over, a puzzled expression on her face, but then nodded in understanding. "Oh right, I forgot you're not old enough to be on this yet, huh?"

"Amma and Appa* say I have to be 13 before I can set up a profile," I answered. "And we're going to have a 'talk' before that happens."

"Well, that actually makes a lot of sense to me," Lucy replied, a thoughtful expression on her face. "Instagram can be a bit complicated."

**Amma and Appa are Korean for Mom and Dad.*

Lucy handed me her phone. “This is my profile, and it’s basically where I share photos and videos from my life. See, I’ve got pictures from my birthday last weekend.”

I kept scrolling through her profile, noticing it was mostly pictures of her goofing around with friends. “But—this is all completely safe, right, Lucy? Amma makes such a big deal about me not being on social media until I’m older.”

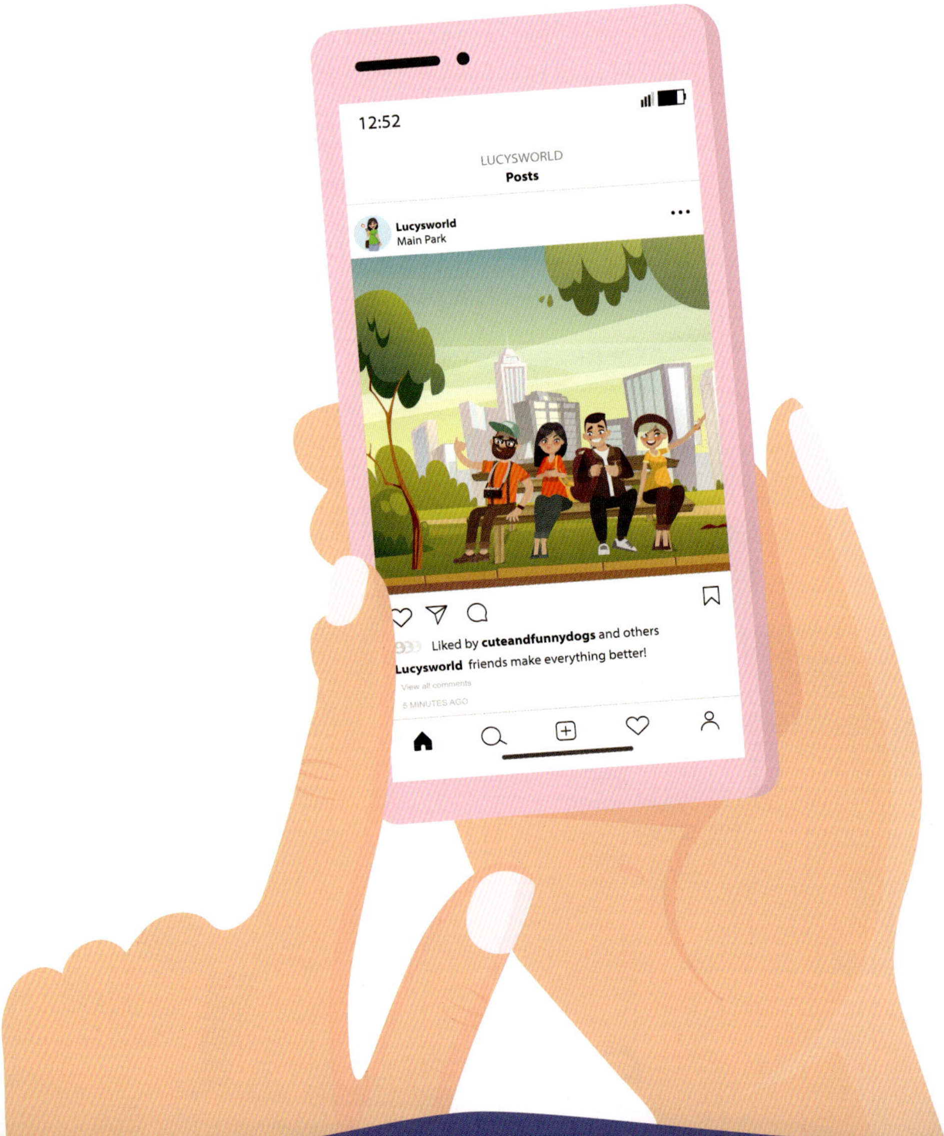

Lucy frowned, deep in thought. "I think there are danger zones with everything. Think about when we go hiking in Yosemite. It's safe, but we have to stay on the marked trails and keep an eye out for anything dangerous, like uneven paths or bears. I think the internet is like that—it's a pretty cool place as long as you go through it carefully."

"How do you do that?" I asked.

"Well, for example, my Instagram profile is private. I only add people I know, so only my friends see my pictures. I also never talk to strangers online. You just need to trust your gut, you know? If something feels off or kind of scary, back away and ask for help from Amma or Appa." Lucy smiled widely at me. "You'll figure it all out—and you always have me as a support system when you're old enough to join the world of social media."

She looped her arm over my shoulder, and I grinned back at her.

Back to Nonfiction

Keep It Private

The online world is a complex network. Billions of people use the internet to find information. But as people **browse** the web, they often share information about themselves. People need to be careful with what they share.

Every person is a collection of **unique** details. We all have a favorite movie. We like certain foods better than others. Our homes are at specific addresses. Different activities fill our weekends. Everyone has a birthday on a certain day. All these personal details make us who we are. If you created a profile about yourself, there'd be a lot of details to include! But while online, it's important to think carefully before sharing details about ourselves. Not all details are safe to share online.

Protecting Children

In 1998, the Children's Online Privacy Protection Act was passed into law. This law helps keep children safe online. It makes rules for websites that are visited by children under 13 years old. The act says what has to be included in a website's privacy policy. It also includes when and how to get a parent's **consent** about collecting a child's personal data.

Social media profiles should not reveal any private data.

Details about who we are fall into two categories. They are personal data and private data. Personal data includes details about our personal lives, such as our favorite sports. But some details about us are meant to stay as private data. Private data includes important details, such as our full names and addresses. While online, the key is to know what kinds of data we are sharing.

Personal vs. Private

People often share details about their personal lives online. Some people do this through social media. People may post pictures about their weekend ski trips. Or someone might share information about a television show they are watching. It is up to each person to decide how much detail to share about their life. Here are a few things to keep in mind before you share.

Security questions require you to answer personal questions.

Think and Talk

What social media accounts do your family members have?

Some of your information should always stay private. This includes details such as your home address and phone number. Another piece of data you should not share online is your date of birth. Sometimes, certain websites may need this information to **verify** your identity. This is true for some health care websites, for example. You can share this information to verify your identity. But make sure you only share it with the help of a trusted adult.

Keep in mind that only a few people live at your address, and your birth date is specific to you. If strangers have access to your private data, your private life becomes more accessible to them. This means they could find your location or steal your identity.

Identity Theft

Sometimes, people steal your data for their own gain. This happens when someone else takes your personal data. They can use it to log in to your accounts. If someone knows details about you, such as your date of birth, they can use those details to change your passwords or possibly even steal from you.

Your Online Reputation

Some details about people are private and should never be shared. As a young person, you have the right to privacy. You also have the right to the protection of your personal data. The government has certain laws in place so that your rights are **upheld**. But you also have a responsibility to think before you share online.

It is up to you to decide what kinds of personal information you share online. Your private details should always stay private. But as social media use rises, people are given a lot of choice as to what they share online. Many people will post about their whole lives online. You can choose to share a lot of details with the digital world.

Follow My "Finsta"

Some people have multiple Instagram accounts. One is their regular account. The second is a smaller, more personal account. *Finsta* is a combination of "fake" and "Insta." Some people have finstas so they can share whatever they want. They may post more private things on their finstas than they would on their regular accounts.

Parents make different choices about the right time for their children to get phones.

Everyone has a **reputation**. This also extends online. People often put a lot of thought into the clothes they wear. They tend to think before they speak. But that same thought is not always put into what people share online.

Information shared online is "sticky." That means others can keep copies of anything shared online. Online information leaves a digital history that cannot be deleted. It is vital to keep that in mind before sharing information you would not want to "stick" around in the future.

Know Your Boundaries

The internet is a public space that many people can access. So, people should always think carefully before they share data online. This means thinking through our online **boundaries**.

Everyone has different boundaries. A boundary helps you define what is OK and what is not OK for you. For instance, we have boundaries around our personal lives. Your friend might feel OK sharing pictures of their family vacation. But another friend may want to keep those memories private.

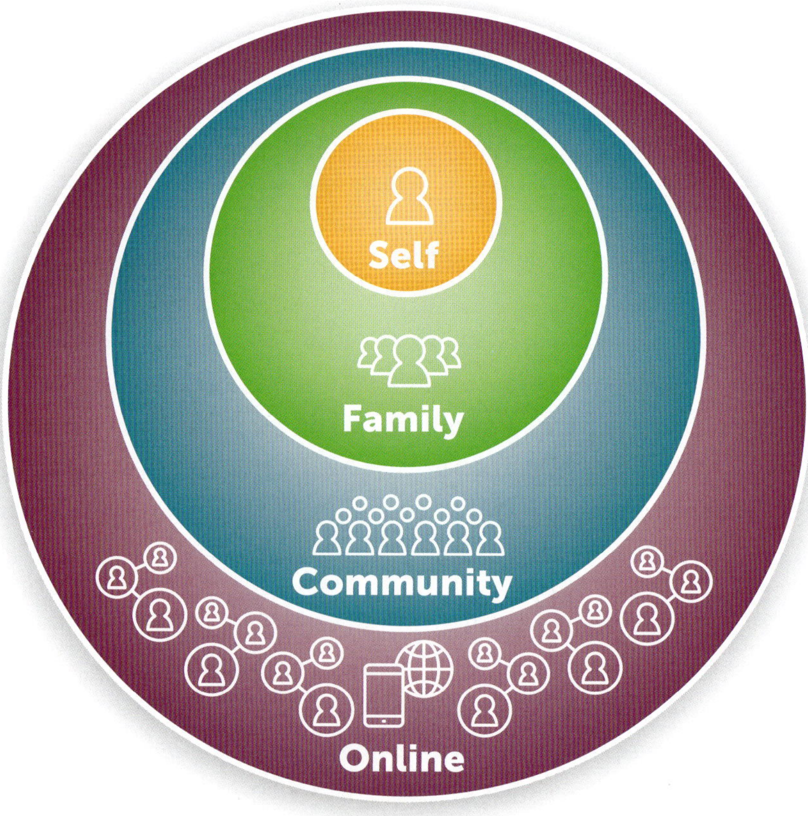

Digital Footprint

Anyone who uses the internet leaves a digital footprint, even if they don't realize it! This footprint refers to the data you leave behind, such as which websites you visit, what information you share with websites, emails you send, or phrases you search for. This is why it's so important to be aware of your actions online.

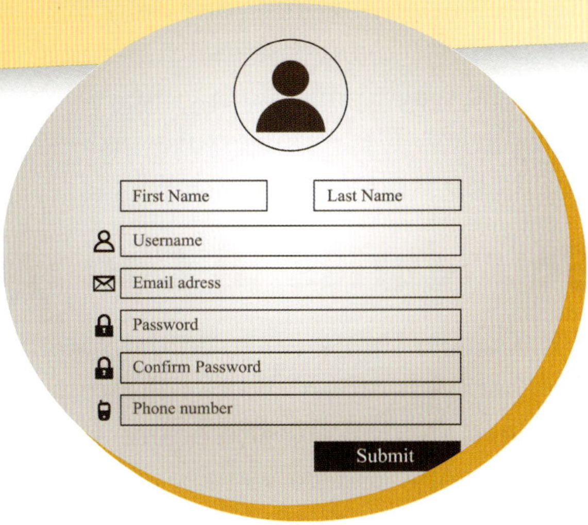

Defining Limits

What are your boundaries, or limits, online? This is a discussion you can have with a trusted adult. For starters, talk about limits around your privacy. What do you want to share online? And what do you want to remain private?

Knowing our boundaries is a good starting point. We can then maintain those limits. For instance, while online, you will likely visit a variety of websites. You might go onto a site to play games or watch videos. Websites may ask you for your name, or they may want you to create an account. If you do not feel comfortable, you do not have to share that information.

Before you share data on any website, you should look through the site's privacy policy. Look for terms such as *personal information*. What does the policy say about storing or sharing your data?

If a company shares your data, you can say *no* to using their site. Saying *no* is one way to maintain your boundaries. It is a powerful word—and it also works as an action.

Boundaries in Connections

It is easier than ever to connect with people online. People can chat with others many time zones away. Language **barriers** are broken with online **translators**. Social media allows people to freely share about their lives. Building connections is a powerful use of the internet.

Online and offline connections are similar. When people connect with others, they often have boundaries. Boundaries help people say what is and is not OK with them. Boundaries help people feel safe within their connections.

When you are online, trust your instincts. If something feels unsafe, say *no* to continuing the connection. Then, touch base with a trusted adult. They can help you figure out how to move forward.

Think and Talk

What online and offline connections do you have?

Crossing Oceans

Have you ever wondered how people can communicate online with people who live far away? It's all thanks in part to underwater cables! Long, thin wires extend across Earth's ocean floors. These wires connect the world. There are almost 750,000 miles (1,207,008 kilometers) of cables around the world!

A Safe Space

As a young person, you have the right to a safe online space. There are government policies in place to ensure that your rights are upheld. But you are also **accountable** for your safety online.

Do you know how to find a safe space online? First, it can help to have a trusted adult provide guidance. Second, check to see if the site's privacy policy is easily available. It should have clear information about how the site collects and shares your data. Third, carefully consider the content and purpose of the site. Does the website contain meaningful content that interests you? And does the site promote respectful **interactions**?

Internet Dependent

Many adults spend a large part of their days online. In 2020, people used the internet for an average of 6 hours and 43 minutes each day! How can you keep track of screen usage? There are apps that track this.

Next, think about how you want to spend your time online. We can have boundaries for ourselves, too. Today, you can browse museums online or use fact-checking tools to verify the articles you read. There are a ton of online games that put your math and science skills to the test. People can check up on what their friends are doing with social media.

Some people feel that they spend too much time on the internet. It's key to remember that there's a world outside of your digital one! Setting guidelines for yourself is helpful to make sure you spend your time wisely.

Pair Freedom with Responsibility

The internet is a wide digital world that we can **navigate**. People engage within this world. Messages between friends are sent back and forth online. Using social media, people can share their opinions on events. After reading articles online, they may respond with their thoughts.

Americans have the right to "freedom of expression." This is the right to share thoughts on decisions that affect their lives. This includes chatting with other people about their views. All Americans may express their views freely. This can be done both offline and online.

People also have a right to build their knowledge online. Access to online information helps them explore new concepts. These rights give people the chance to learn more about the world—and their place in it.

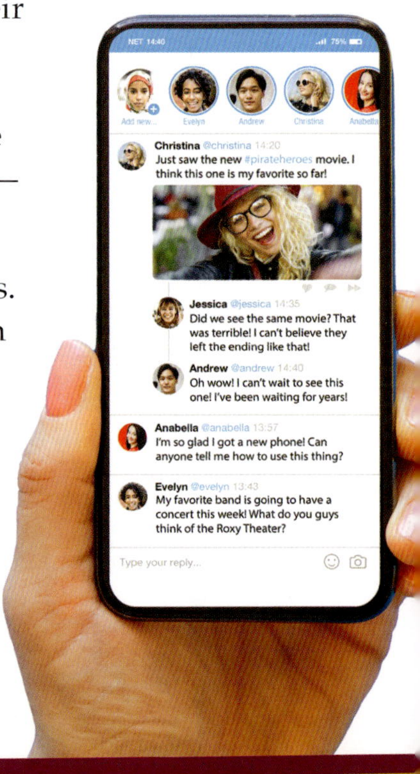

But people also have responsibilities. Eleanor Roosevelt said, "With freedom comes responsibility." People have the right to their own views. And they are also responsible for respectfully engaging with others. This includes online interactions.

Eleanor Roosevelt

Freedom as a Tool

Eleanor Roosevelt, former First Lady of the United States, was a leader for human rights and freedoms. In a 1948 speech to the United Nations, she said, "Freedom of speech, freedom of the press, freedom of information, freedom of assembly... they are tools with which we create a way of life, a way of life in which we can enjoy freedom."

Combat Cyberbullying

The digital world is a platform for many interactions. Messaging online is a simple way to keep in contact with friends who live far away. People can use social media to speak up about topics that matter to them. Thoughtful debates about big issues can rise up between strangers. It's easier than ever to have a voice online.

It is important to understand the **impact** of our words. Our voices can be used to shed light on issues. We can spread awareness of topics that matter to us. But we also must remember our audience. While interacting with people online, we are typing words onto a screen. It can be easy to forget that people just like us are on the other side. Sometimes, people post comments that are deeply hurtful to others. Online chats might turn into an exchange of cruel words. **Trolls** can share nasty, upsetting messages and images.

Over half of American teenagers have been victims of cyberbullying. They may have been called **offensive** names or may have been the focus of rumors. Online bullying is a serious issue for many young people.

Catfishing

Sometimes, people lie about who they are online. They may use another person's images to create false profiles. They chat with other people using fake identities. This is known as *catfishing*.

HA.HA..
loser!
!!!
cancelled!

Everyone can expect respect online. Remember, you have the right to feel safe while on the internet. If you or your friends are bullied online, you can say *no* to the interaction. Reach out to a trusted adult to talk about what happened. Addressing the issue starts with speaking up.

People have a responsibility to others. Treating other people fairly and kindly is key. This is true for both our in-person and online connections. Anything you would not say to someone's face should not be said online.

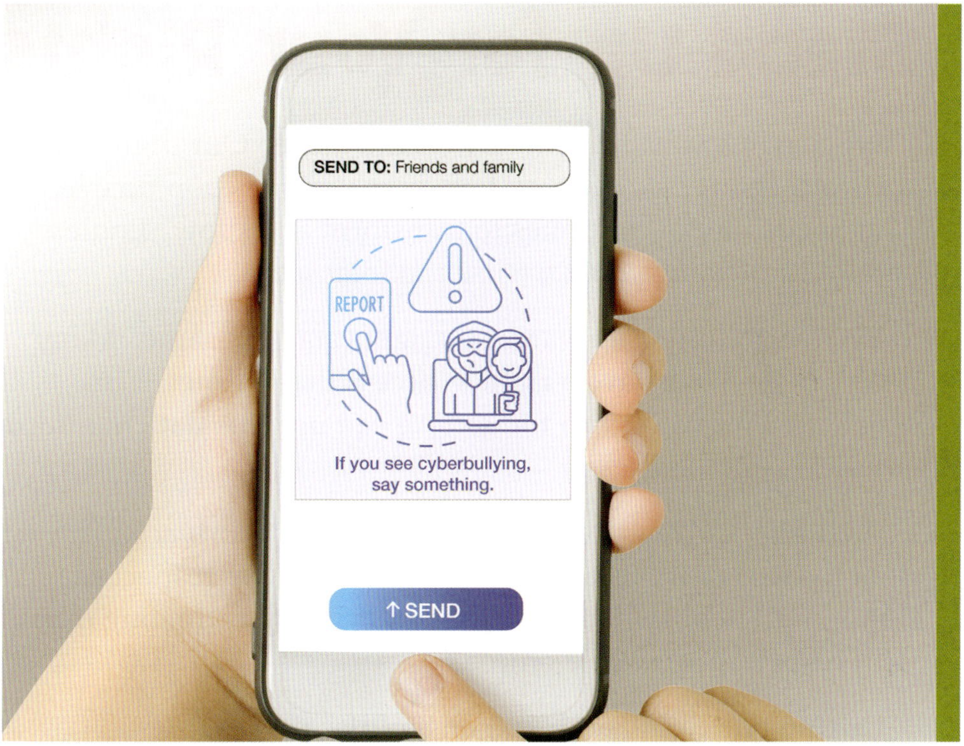

Being a Digital Citizen

Connecting with other people is a powerful use of the internet. While using the internet, keep in mind that we are all digital citizens. There is a lot of data online, but not all of it is correct. We need to make sure we fact-check information before we share it.

Americans have the right to freely express their views. But they also have a responsibility to share accurate facts. Researching your views is part of being a responsible citizen. Everyone has the right to have their own views. Respecting the rights of others is also crucial. Being a digital citizen means standing up for your rights and the rights of others.

Stand Up for Your Rights

We live in a world constantly on the move. Our digital world is always changing. New and creative websites pop up every day. Social media continues to transform and grow. Endless possibilities change how we use the internet.

Even as we move forward, our rights stay the same. Many people believe we have a right to access the internet. This opens up a world of data for us. We can use this data to inform our views and choices.

As digital citizens, we also have the right to privacy. The right to free speech is also key. It's vital that we respect the rights of all people. Part of our responsibility is treating others with respect, even while online.

Pairing our rights with responsibilities makes for **upstanding** digital citizens. The internet contains an exciting and vast world of data. Knowing our rights online ensures we can find our way around this world safely—and respectfully.

Ask for Permission

Cell phones make it easier than ever for people to take pictures and videos. But people do not have the right to take pictures and videos of anyone, anywhere, anytime. Always ask permission before you start recording and before you post anything online.

Glossary

access—to be able to use or get something

accountable—required to be responsible for something

barriers—things that make it difficult for people to understand one another

boundaries—limits that define acceptable behavior

browse—to find and look at information on the internet

consent—agreement

data—information that is produced or stored by a computer

impact—a powerful or major influence or effect

interactions—the acts of talking or doing things with other people

navigate—to go to different places on the internet or on a particular website in order to find what you want

offensive—rude or insulting

reputation—overall quality or character of something as seen or judged by other people

translators—websites that change words written in a language into a different language

trolls—people on the internet who intentionally try to upset others with offensive messages or images

unique—unlike anything or anyone else

upheld—supported or defended

upstanding—honest and respectable

verify—to prove or show that something is true or correct

Index

American(s), 22, 24, 27

boundaries, 16–18, 21

catfishing, 24

Children's Online Privacy Protection Act (COPPA), 10

cyberbullying, 24

digital citizen(s), 27–28

freedom, 22–23

freedom of expression, 22

identity theft, 13

Instagram, 6–7, 9, 14

internet, 4–5, 9–10, 16, 18, 20–22, 26–28

messaging, 4, 24

online reputation, 14–15

personal data, 10–11, 13–14

privacy policy, 10, 18, 20

private data, 11

profile(s), 7–11, 24

right(s), 5, 14, 20, 22–23, 26–28

Roosevelt, Eleanor, 22–23

safe space, 20

social media, 8–9, 11–12, 14, 18, 21–22, 24, 28

United Nations, 23

Civics in Action

Most people use the internet a lot. They may not even think about what they do online. They may be sharing more information than they should. It's a good idea to stop and reflect. You can help people in your school to do that.

1. Work with your classmates to create a survey about online activities.
2. Give the survey to students, faculty, and staff at your school.
3. Review the results.
4. Share the information, and encourage people to reflect on what they do online.